LAW OF THE HIMYARITES

Gregentios
Bishop of Taphar

Translated by: D.P. Curtin

LAW OF THE HIMYARITES

Copyright @ 2024 Dalcassian Press

All rights reserved. No part of this publication may be reproduced, distributed, or transmitted in any form or by any means, including photocopying, recording, or other electronic or mechanical methods, without the prior written permission of the publisher, except in the case of brief quotations embodied in critical reviews and certain other non-commercial uses permitted by copyright law. For permission request, write to Dalcassian Press at dalcassianpublishing at gmail.com

ISBN: 979-8-3302-5305-0 (Paperback)

Library of Congress Control Number:
Author: Curtin, D.P. (1985-)

Printed by Ingram Content Group, 1 Ingram Blvd, La Vergne, Tennessee

First printing edition 2024.

LAW OF THE HIMYARITES
Gregentios, Bishop of Taphar

God's wisdom and understanding, which is holy, powerful, with an eye that looks upon the poor, asking that we just let them see Him, with your eyes always watching over all those assembled before his face. Who is worthy of your design? We must pursue the good, as it will glorify Your most holy name.

With these things prayed for, and with hope in our virtue, the Lord will proceed forth in spirit and join us. It was decided in the presence of the eunuchs, and Elesbaa the king. When they all saw this sign, they, admirably, withdrew and cried out in astonishment: Kyrie Elison!

The very famous bishop truly answered, saying to the king: "that which you, my most pious king, have shown by your right hand, return it forth, my brother. Likewise, forgive the misdeed in others, that the Lord may make use of it successfully, so that by the love of Christ we may receive grace."

The king, not delaying for a moment, put on his tunic and immediately went forth. He took for himself the crown of his kingdom and put it on his head, along with the shoes upon his feet. Truly, they arrived at the cathedral, built in the name of the Trinity as a sanctuary, so that they might participate in the divine sacrifice and the procession of those things holy. They went to the entrance, to the divine altar, altogether with that most pious king, Elesbaa

When his duty was dispatched, they proclaimed with joy to the army: "Elesbaa, the most holy king of the Ethiopians, may he have many happy years!" And they repeated this seven times, before exclaiming: "Abram, the lover of Christ, king of the Himyarites, the greatest of the pious, may he have many years." He was, therefore, a junior to the king, and all those present said this again, "good fortune to both of them." They subsequently said "Elesbaa and Abram the most pious. Let there be many years for the king! Gregentios, the most holy archbishop, our pacific shepherd, may he be healthy and whole. May he have many good and holy years!" The king prayed for the good fortune of the army, having just returned to the palace of the kings, and had a magnificent banquet offered for all there, eating in cleanliness with the whole of the army.

Elesbaa remained most righteous, therefore, just as Abram, the lover of Christ, and king of the Himyarites, had established himself in that region for thirty-three days. He laid the foundations for everything beautiful there, and would admonish the king, Abram, for the need to rule the kingdom with piety. He did this in accordance with the customs of the bedouin. He also carried church books with the army, escorted by five thousand Ethiopian soldiers, leaving because of the siege.

The king then moved his military camp to Ethiopia, and returned there in safety, giving thanks to God. He gave neither gold, nor silver, nor any precious stones or pearls, but made his offering and washed himself. He offered his adoration to God, along with his subjects, and did so repeatedly.

He was betrayed in his own kingdom by his own son, Atherphotham, who was clothed in a hair shirt. In the mountains, Orpha said, "the clouds of heaven are coming close, for we are abiding here in the desert". There he went down into a dark hut beneath the earth, and closed the way to all those who approached the cave. He said "All of my life I did not wish to see by day, nor do I wish to speak with anyone except the angels in this life. And so, I go the Lord, with the pure and penitent I will eat. He was therefore accepted amongst the monks who abide in holes. He sought to bring something forth from the lower mountain before returning.

Among the many things that were said about the monastery is that there was a brother there who left the monastery, committed fornication and drinking wine in great abundance, indulging himself. He went to return there one day, and he had been alone after what he had done. He went through the desert, attempting to return to the monastery, walking along the precarious cliff face. When suddenly, without any warning, a serpents of unusual size jumped up before him trying to persecute and kill him. But he fled from that place and was not deceived by him.

He was pursued closer by that serpent and felt he could not do anything to prevent himself from collapsing and being devoured. He fled with happiness, and thought of Elesbaa, and looked back at the serpent saying: "I plead with thee, by the most holy and just king, Elesbaa, depart from me, and do not pursue me any longer." Indeed, the serpent revered the name which was implored by the monk. The serpent answered him with a human voice, "I say to you, how will I spare you for a moment, for an angel of the Lord commanded me from my heart to devour you, because of your fornication. And, because the service of the Lord compels me, did you not cease to defile your body, and grieve the Holy Ghost of God?" Yet, the man who stood there and heard this was astonished because he spoke as if he was a man and trembled as before he asked for help. He spoke again, answering, saying to the serpent, "Swear, my son, that henceforth you will not assume unclean desire. You must not indulge in the first accident of the world, my son, for this you will be safe and I will leave you." The monk swore saying, "By him that dwelleth in heaven, the Lord, and by the veneration of the holy king, Elesbaa's name, I must say that I am not my own master. He would be frustrated, just as you are, that I was out being sinful according to the flesh, living in lust." As this was happening, the conversation between the serpent and the monk, fire fell from the heavens, and the serpent went before the monk he tried to devour, who shook with fear and fled into the monastery from which he had come. He no longer continued to sin in the sight of the Lord, but his life ended in repentance.

And this was true, indeed, of the most blessed company, and in truly the most pious king Elesbaa, who had all of the priests of the churches be brought forth. Among the wisest of them he chose a bishop and ordered him to rule over the city. He commanded this together with the most illustrious king, Abram, and all those that were under his dominionship and of their own vain religion to be baptized, or exiled, or if they persisted, to be hung by a rope.

His edict was, therefore, promulgated among the men, who with their wives and children, accepted the divine rebirth through baptism in a hurry, and through it proceeded to Christ. They were baptized for all of the bishops to see and went forth throughout the city with a pure disposition, for there were many illuminated people, and many devils were exiled.

When they were done all of this, many were baptized and had come to the knowledge of the truth. And yet, this excited and Jews from all over the kingdom and of the city. They met with each other by means of a council, and said to themselves, "What shall we do to be able to survive? For unless we let them baptize us under the king's edict, the soldiers will kill us, for disagreeing with the royal court again." And with hopes for a plan, knowing there would be others, they said, "Let us do it, and obey the will of the king, so that we might not die before our time, and in secret ignore such a faith." Others, however, said, "True, if we did this, would we be able to? God will see the law that would will have violated. God will, therefore, take revenge and retribution on us for this action. And we will perish all the more." Others said, "Now we no longer need God, since our pious king Dunaan Elesha will deliver us from their hands, so that we will not be killed by the army. Let us go there right away stealthily, so that we might not be taken from this country. Let us depart therefore, less our souls be separated from our bodies." Others also said, "But what if we want to migrate in this way, the one in which you spoke, and these

Christians know these things? They will know the evil that we plainly host and discover it."

One of them, whose name was Herbanus, was a doctor of the law, eloquent and very cunning, skilled in the Old Testament. And so, he answered them, "You are all vain. You think that this all means nothing, that it has been arranged and brought before you. What if you all wish to agree to this? Immediately the king and Gregentios the bishop will demand to choose some men to argue with us. So that, if indeed, we were forced by speech to persuade them, from the heart of the Christian, a sentence of the flame. But if we do not persuade them, it is obvious they will interfere with our faith in our failure. Why then? We know what it is like, let it be their faith. For if it is true, we would believe it. Do we not know? Perhaps, the messiah has already come and we were not ignorant. Yet, if untruths are found, we shall know the reason why God has let us die, and we will sharply embrace death.

 Altogether, Onines and Herbanus, fearing a riot said: "We have seen that you too are Christians. The true faith is ours; don't you know? How will we leave it?" Herbanus said, "Speak no evil, brothers. Be aware that we know where he is going, and the reason for forced baptism. If you go off to be believers, I have no sorrow for you. Finally, in good faith, I have not experienced what you have, and you will believe without seeing it, as those who have been ordered have done so. Yet, you will not believe anyone who flees from us, for they will died, killed by our hands, before we will go and die." And having said this, they all agreed with Herbanus.

So they all wrote in a book his arguments, which they had written and given to the king to confirm. They hoped that he would open and that he would read it and become enraged and try to kill them. However, in humility, he brought forth the archbishop, and the document which he had been given. The archbishop said that it was a very good thing to have, and the king agreed in happiness. It was said to the king, "They are right. The Jews will not accept this from their heart, and they will not truly believe. Without arguing with them, we will give them what they seek, and if we are able to convince them to be baptized, then they will refuse their plea, and they will be brought into Christ's kingdom." Upon hearing this, the king gave them forty days to offer a response, so that they might deliberate for a time and choose someone that they might be able to send forth to discuss things.

Therefore, they sent someone out into the places of their country, and asked the men there who they should meet, so that they might go before the king and discuss things. When this was finished, therefore, at the aforesaid time, the most blessed flock put forth a just plan to the most pious king, that he might consult with his council, and issue his orders piously. "Command", he said "O king, leaders of each region that are elected as being secondary, and all royals of the Himyarite state as being first. So that all of your kingdom, and of its states, they will send forth their nobles, and it will be established by them, thus avoiding having to make any decision in writing."

Therefore, the king numbered some thirty-one regions, the first of which was the royal city of Nijran and sent quickly to each of these regions' governors. He placed them over them and commanded all thirty-one to obtain the proper platform in their provinces, in a space that would occupy the middle of a marketplace. He therefore had this inscribed in all the houses of government, so that they might exercise their role and command control. Moreover, so that they might know the limits of their authority, and not err by extending themselves into another domain, looking to establish order. And to these officials, he gave them command over sixteen soldiers. With this, the king also ordered to grant them stipends, bounties, and mercantile gifts, and to act with prudence and the fear of God. He also ordered the most blessed collection of writings, so that they would do with them as he had suggested, and to know to avoid those things that should be avoided. He himself ordered that this should be carried out from the beginning, and it mediated calm minds and happiness.

And yet, the king sought to help the old, the sick, and the needy, and offered strangers his hospitality immediately. He did many things for them. And from the tenants of those in his townships, which he had been founded by Dunanus, the king of the Hebrews, and his nobles, he found the needy, the old, and infirm in want. He found the lame and the blind, and he magnificently took care of them, restoring their state, providing them with wages through the year, along with clothes, food, wine, oil, and fruit. He provided them with goods of every race, and as such, his fame and praise were comparable to that of the patriarch Abraham, or that of Job, who ruled previously, because of the hospitality of his mind, and his infinite beneficence. For when he was celebrating the memory of the saints, he placed two tables of edits, one for the needy, and the other for himself. At the hour of supper, he made a table for the needy, and he was always eating among them. And to everyone he presented the most magnificent gifts. If anyone asked something good from him, he would offer it to them immediately. He listened to their need, and to them freely. When he came to the end of his reign, there was no one poor with the kingdom that could be found, nor was there any injustice under the law, nor anyone suffering from any injury. And God collected all of the people around him. For this, in all of his days, war did not break out, but only a deep peace, joy, and charity. He had diligence for the care of the poor, for the widow and the orphan, for the protections allotted for unspoken justice, for the great feasts of the church and their unique constitution.

For divine worship, however, he wrote the law that St. Gregentios, as if he was the king himself, was to create what follows in this narrative. To this, it was issued forth:

When Our Redeemer and Almighty God, through his limitless kindness, raised us to this high place over many other men, in consulting with our own worthiness, he placed us at the pinnacle of power. It befits us, as his benefactor, that we thank him with this act, and also with this, that we act in strength, love, and power to serve him. Because of neither dignity or glory, he has kindly awakened us, as the most excellent head of the Himyarite government, to the act of charity, true as it is. With sincerity and submission, with fear and trembling, and eagerness from him to establish these laws so that they might be quickly carried out. We are committed to doing this enterprise very well, not only at the present moment, but also in the future. Indeed, just as God revealed to Moses his commandments and laws at the time of the exodus from Egypt, he said these things about the people: "If I hear your will, be it heard from the voice, Lord our God, so that is rightly done. All of the wrath which was taken upon us in Egypt be brought upon us." Therefore, just as the Egyptians before, let us recognize the threat, and keep his commandments in rightful fear.

THE BEGINNING OF THE LAW

Chapter I. Therefore, we order our meekness and our mercy to those who rule over their neighbors. From this royal decree they are to receive the cities of the metropolis with tremendous authority, especially those of this city and its foundations. In hopes of composing the greatest order, I wish this to be done to establish law in our city. We command this, but we recognize the subjects of our power, if they are cautious, let them respect all as they sit down as they equal in public. By humility, they may be given places that are secured as common grounds- city streets, roads, village squares, public houses, marketplaces, so that they might secure bread and wine, and whatever they might need. And in each country, we will reserve this for the faithful. And another will be reserved for the neighbor who does not look to his own management, but to the governance we command. We commit each to their own rules as we wish.

Chapter II. Be careful not to be hasty in a manslaughter case. If it has happened, the killer will be arrested immediately, and be delivered into the power of the local magistrate. Observe those who have committed adultery, incest, beastiality. If anyone has committed such a crime, and if they have admitted to it, bring them to the magistrate.

Chapter III. Be careful with the ugly lust of the Sodomites. If anyone is caught as such, he should be arrested and brought before the magistrate, following this let the law be raged against them. Yet, it is not for them to be killed, living in the stink of sin and their own abomination. For this reason, I will say, they might still defile other immaculate souls of the innocent, and the wrath of God will be upon us for the uncleanliness that they will incite.

Chapter IV. Do not look to perform magic, either through potions or through incantations. If anyone has been discovered doing this, take them immediately to the magistrate, so that such a crime will be delivered up by fire, where the admitted are burned. Look to see that it is not taken on account of prestige, or by false testimony. If anyone has done as such, if he dates, let him be handed over to the magistrate, so that his tongue may be cut off at once.

Chapter V. Be vigilant, very vigilant, and diligently pay attention to thieves, and those who receive or hide the belongings that they stole. The first offense brings with its fifty clubs, with whips, and with fines, and finally with a sign, that is a seal of iron burnt on their front. Thus, before all of the dressed people, let him go naked. Say to them "Be careful brothers, for from this theft onwards, you will not be arrested twice." If anyone again commits a similar crime and is discovered (which will be easier with their brand), he will be brought to the magistrate, and cut his right foot off and let him go as if it were stolen as he willed. He will not be able to stand on his one foot and will be unable to walk. Then he will be among the entertainment for the poor of our kingdom, as from then on, every day of life he must beg for food.

Chapter VI. Every husband, and all the women are to avoid the unclean act of fornication, and therefore must have a spouse. Let it be to them a beautiful defense against this, and say: "I have always been poor, and a wife I cannot have." To this we answer, "If you do not want to join yourself in a legitimate marriage, we will not compel you. But be careful that you do not sin even with your own skin. If this is to be found, it is immediately perilous." It is commanded for the humility of our kingdom, anyone caught in fornication, male or female, that they should receive one hundred clubs, accepting the blow of the whips. Then their right ear shall be cut off. Finally, a notice of their offense will be printed. Equally, any woman who has no husband, and is caught as such, she will be affected in the same manner. If a man is caught not having a wife, with a woman who does not have a husband, they will thereafter be united in marriage, living calmly and wisely, and have this administered by a priest, and thereafter these two are to be released.

Chapter VII. If a man is found to have overpowered a woman, immediately the body part which he commits the sin should be cut off. Also, the left mammary of a woman, for it belongs abandoned by her husband, mixed with that of Satan. It is worth, says the Lord, that one part of his body should perish, rather than his whole body be sent to the fire.

Chapter VIII. Whoever is lawfully married, and having left for another, he commits fornication, the part of his sin may be cut off. However, if a spouse discovers this and says, "I do not attribute that to my husband's sin. Even if he defrauded me six hundred times, I want only that of my own impunity. "Let him give to the man two hundred lashes of the flames, and cut off his left ear, and give it to his wife and it has been written out.

Chapter IX. This should be the same for the adulterous woman. If she is a mother, her ears are to be cut offered to her husband. If after this, the same woman gives birth, and they have been caught, they will submit to the former punishment as well. And then, if this happens again, that such a woman is caught committing such an act, then whipping will have no effect, she should be expelled from the city.

Chapter X. If a rich man wishes to marry a poor woman he has fallen in love with, and his parents refuse this, showing no pity for their rejection, then the law should unite them in marriage. This should be established by the parents with their son's dowry intact, just as the royal order commands. The same is also true of the rich woman and the poor young man.

Chapter XI. It should follow the book that marriage is not possible between a master and mistress and the slave that serves them. The same is also true of a free woman, that she must not submit herself to a slave. For all of the members of Christ, this is the making of a harlot. He is a man's servant who flatters him with as much evil as sin.

Chapter XII. Each man we command to properly have but one wife, and to flee from and abhor fornication. For this is how the wrath of God came upon us from the winds to the children of men. Those who do these things have had their transgressions manifested and should hear the punishment that should be paid.

Chapter XIII. It is commanded by God, for the authority of the king, that parents must not let their own children into marriage until they are from ten to twelve years of age. This is the truth of the law, and if violators are present, they will pay six gold pounds in the country of their magistrate. However, if they are middle class, three gold pieces in minor cases, or one and a half otherwise. If they are poor, a fine of one pound for those who seek a fine, thirty-six coins after this, then eighteen, then nine, then four and a half. After these two and three coins, then one and a sixth part, and then a half. And then they do not wait for the call, but they will be ordered to pay this time. If they are waiting to do so, and he refuses to do so, he may be banished.

Chapter XIV. We command that whoever violates the divine and peaceful commands of our majesty, according to their abilities, as prescribed, shall be punished. The prefect of the region where the offenses are committed shall receive those who are repelled by him, along with the soldiers accompanying him.

Chapter XV. If anyone observes their neighbor engaging in a wrongful and unjust business, and does not warn the prefect of their region, and if they are caught, if wealthy, they shall receive seventy-two lashes in public; if poor, four gold coins; if of lesser means, three; if of even lower status, two; and if completely destitute, one coin shall be imposed.

Chapter XVI. If anyone acts as a messenger for adulterers or arranges the most impure union of boys or eunuchs, with whom the foolish, insane, and impious are accustomed to commit wickedness, whether male, female, or of any other identity. And if this person is caught doing such things, we order that half of his tongue be cut off, so that if he wishes to serve Satan in the future, like the serpent once did in paradise, he will not be able to do so through his tongue. For these wicked ones are cursed because with the empty words of their lips they deceive people as if they were insane, and they deliver them to the devil for the destruction of their souls.

Chapter XVII. Those who turn their homes into houses of fornication, and engage in wickedness in them, should be caught and brought before the authorities with all their possessions, and expelled from the city, with a written pledge that they will no longer engage in such activities, and they shall live away from public affairs for the rest of their lives. Our kindness does not allow the ministers of demons to be present in the cities under our rule. Just as the worst devil has long ago persecuted through idolatrous kings the beloved and worshippers of our Lord Jesus Christ and has taken away our pure faith from the face of the Christians on earth, it has seemed fitting to remove all the displays of that dragon's malice and wickedness from our power by persecuting them through believers in Christ.

Chapter XVIII. But we, fulfilling the oath that God swore to our father Abraham, decree that we will not cease all our lives from bringing countless evils upon all those who practice wickedness and trample underfoot this law given to us by God, unless they cease from sinning. If not, we will not refrain from destroying them. For the wondrous David, achieving similar things to these, responded to the world: In the morning I will destroy all the sinners of the land, that I may destroy from the city of the Lord all who work iniquity.

Chapter XIX. Those who attack women on the road and commit violence against them, like enemies of God and thieves, convicted by the woman herself with an oath, around. Let them receive a hundred lashes with a stick, and let each ear be cut off, and then let them be released. And if, after this, they are found doing the same thing, let them be expelled after suffering two hundred lashes.

Chapter XX. If anyone, while passing through the marketplace or street, shamefully lays hands on passing women with a bacchic and dishonorable desire, in the presence of some onlookers, and with the woman crying out, let such a man be fined with two hundred and seventy lashes in the middle of the marketplace before the people, and after being publicly shamed and receiving a warning, let him be released. But if he is caught doing the same thing again, let his hands be cut off as a most shameless act. For our leniency dictates that one should have their own spouse, and not lay hands on another, nor wink at them if possible.

Chapter XXI. For our royal empire does not allow Christians who are fornicators, adulterers, sodomites, sorcerers and enchanters, or similar offenders, to dwell in the kingdom. For this reason, God sent his wrath upon us from heaven, to crush and destroy us in our sins. Therefore, we do not succeed prosperously in the battles because of these sins, for the weapons of war, it is said, are justice; and if my people had listened to me, if Israel had walked in my ways, I would have humbled their enemies as nothing, and I would have sent my hand against those who trouble them, says God. So let all wickedness and iniquity be removed from our midst, and let all virtue, justice, and truth be exalted, so that the Lord our God may subject to us the nations that surround us.

Chapter XXII. We do not command a man falsely accused by the Lord to defend himself in any action, unless he has first received protection according to the law, when questioned about the law, as the law commands. But those who dare to do so from this day forward, whether they be of noble birth, rich or poor, informers, officials, members of our society, soldiers, or any others subject to our authority, namely to beat, slap, kick, or punish anyone with a stick or lashes, whether justly or unjustly, at will, whether in court, or on the street, or at home. Except for those teaching doctrines and arts with letters, and also if a master kills his slave, or a father his son or daughter, and indeed for a just cause; nor should those inclined to anger, desiring to teach, kill a person. And we command the prefects of the city region, being taught such things, to demand written pledges with their own hand, in which they promise not to teach. Therefore, if they are found to be transgressing and adulterating our command, and beating or striking simple and moderate people with force, they shall receive thirty-six strokes of the whip; and one of their toes shall be cut off; and publicly warned, they shall be released, so that they may know how much pain one slap, one whipping, inflicts, just as this one suffered from the sole of his own body's finger. For our royal authority desires all to be sheep of Christ and God, not quarreling, not shouting, not venomous beasts that devour one another.

Chapter XXIII. You are not allowed to beat a man similar to yourself. Therefore, do not beat them, lest you provoke them to anger. You are a man of some importance; do not rely on the splendid dignity of your master to strike a blow to the head of a poor person. Whether you are a member of our group or an informer, do not strike them unless the law commands it. If you are rich and have suffered an injustice, seek refuge in the law and then seek revenge. You are powerful: do good, not evil. If you are poor, do not strike a fellow poor person. If you have suffered an injustice, appear before the judges; and if you are not reconciled, come to us, and we will find someone for you to meet; and thus I will confirm your judgment, if it is right for you.

Chapter XXIV. We do not allow a man to beat his own wife. For adulterers come to the house in the middle of the night, and, accusing the woman of delay, unable to bear her reproach, they begin to beat her. If the woman is also an adulteress, we do not allow the man to beat her either; but we write: Let the accuser report her to the court. And if she is found in her sin, being one of the adulterous women, let her suffer the penalties according to the law. But if anyone is found violating the command of our royal authority, and if he is wealthy, let him receive thirty-six strokes with a rod, and after receiving the warning, let him be dismissed; but if he is poor, let him be fined according to his ability. And if they dare to do the same again after this, let them be brought forward as violators of the royal command, and let their goods, if they are of lower value, be divided by the regional prefect with the soldiers following him; but if they are of high value, let them be handed over to the royal steward. And let them be banished from the city.

Chapter XXV. But a person who is excessively drunk, whether a man or a woman, walking through the marketplace, staggering on their feet, and frequently bumping into walls, shall be seized, confined, and kept until the next morning. And when their drunkenness has been examined, let them be taken out and receive sixty lashes; but thirty if it is a woman; and after being warned, let them be released. For it is written that the drunkards will not inherit the kingdom of God.

Chapter XXVI. Let them observe their yokes or themselves by loading them with heavy and difficult burdens. Those who are caught shall receive thirty-six lashes and be released after being warned. For a strong mule should carry twelve measures, a weaker one ten, and a donkey eight; but if it is even weaker, six. Let them bear the burdens in this way. For it is written: "The righteous have mercy on the souls of their animals, but the hearts of the wicked are cruel."

Chapter XXVII. On the Lord's Day, or the feast of the Lord, we command that nothing else be sold except what is beneficial for the food of men or animals; the rest should be omitted. Whoever transgresses this command, whatever he proposes, besides food as prescribed above, let him lose it, and let him be expelled. But whatever is bought, whether an animal, ox, sheep, or any other large living animal, besides those that are slaughtered in the market, and birds that are sold, whether clothing or anything else. Except for the barley, let all these things be allowed to the governor of the region and the soldiers surrounding him.

Chapter XXVIII. If anyone carries a burden on the great festivals, or on the holy and Christian Lord's Day, besides food, and travels to a distant region, whether by ship, by himself, or by animal, let the burden, if any, and the animal with the burden be brought, and let him be beaten and expelled, because, being a Christian, he has treated the festival no differently than a Jew.

Chapter XXIX. Therefore, our divinity does not want anyone to sell, carry a burden, dig, work, or do anything on the holy Lord's Day, or on the solemn and great feasts of the Lord, or collect taxes, or on the feasts of the Mother of God, or of the twelve holy apostles of our God and Christ and Savior, or of the other saints. However, I leave these matters to our discretion. But those who transgress, having sold the brought items, and having been stripped, shall receive about twenty-four lashes and be pardoned.

Chapter XXX. Those who, because of the presence of magistrates or the king, throw half the legitimate and necessary price at the food sellers, and, by force, snatch what belongs to the poor merchants, and while on their journey, are beaten when calling for help, if caught doing these things, shall receive about twelve strokes with a stick and be publicly admonished. For our royal authority does not allow us to have fraudsters, unjust people, and robbers as ministers. If you want to offer a fair price, do so, take it and continue on your way.

Chapter XXXI. Therefore, we establish the law: Whoever is found in such insolence, after being taught and publicly warned, and after this, having used such things once, if caught again, we order that this man be confined in the public workshop of our kingdom, and work there for four months alongside the laborers. For just as he foolishly and violently attacked, so he must be taught. And let him be released, having experienced the same labor in obtaining his bread as the poor.

Chapter XXXII. Those who engage in a fight in our region, and those who are caught in the marketplace, shall all receive forty lashes, because they dared to inflict excessive violence on each other, either with a club or in any other way. But if one party restrained itself, respected the law, did not raise its hand in defense, and was robbed by the opponent and somehow beaten, then indeed he should be let go as if innocent; but whoever attacked him, whoever he may be, should receive eighty blows, then the public workshop of our kingdom should be closed for two months and then reopened.

Chapter XXXIII. Animals that are being led or loaded, or unloaded, or any other livestock, if they seem to be cruelly beating them, should receive thirty strokes of the stick in their place; for they will understand through their pain how bitter it is to be beaten. Indeed, animals, even though they do not interact or speak, are affected by pain just like us. It is clear from this that those who do not have compassion for their own animals will not have compassion for humans either.

Chapter XXXIV. Those who shamelessly wear fur garments and roam the city streets in a lewd and revealing manner, embracing the vile dominion of Satan and erasing the Christian name, and openly renouncing that oath: I renounce Satan and all his works, shall receive two hundred lashes, and be thrown into the fire, whether it be their hair or beard, and publicly warned that such men should be taken to the royal workshop, and dedicate themselves to work for a whole year, whether they are slaves or free, so that they may learn to walk in piety and fear of God from now on, and not be participants in the works of idolaters, lest they ruin their own souls.

Chapter XXXV. Harpists, lyre players, tragedians, and those who play instruments with their fingers, as well as dancers, whether men or women, young boys or girls. For in the days of our piety and of our kingdom, we do not tolerate such things to be done, nor from anyone who crosses our path. For in every city and region subject to our rule, we do not want there to be either a harpist, or a lyre player, or a tragedian or a dancer, whether man or woman, young man or young woman, neither small nor great. However, we all desire to be good and pious, and to fear the Lord. But whoever wants to rejoice with a calm mind, let them sing. But I do not know how to sing, he says. You have learned the wicked songs of the demon, not written in any book; but you do not learn the psalmody prescribed by God!

Chapter XXXVI. We do not want any tragedian, finger-snapper, dancer, or any kind of impure and shameful play to take place in the land of our kingdom. Transgressors shall be apprehended, beaten, and subjected to flames, that is, fumigation, and publicly rebuked, condemned to work for the entire year in the royal workshop.

Chapter XXXVII. Let those who play dice, who engage in debauched and lascivious dances, and those who pretend to do so, suffer the same fate, we do not prescribe throwing them all unless indeed some are often stirred by the mind and hand to moderation, such as triclinium and similar things.

Chapter XXXVIII. We command those who want to be exalted to strive for this spiritually in the holy churches, namely through prayer, readings, psalmody, and almsgiving. In these things, all should rejoice, as true Christians, as servants of Christ, as children of light, as heirs of the kingdom of colors, praying to leave the house of the Lord, praying to enter the house of God with joy, loving one another, and shining with virtues like the sun.

Chapter XXXIX. Those who provoke each other with insults and reproaches, when captured, shall receive twenty-four strokes of the cane, whether they are male or female. But if anyone casts insults at another and as if throwing a javelin, then indeed, because of the fear of our precept, not responding at all, he instead flees to the magistrate, let him who inflicted the injury receive forty-eight lashes, and publicly rebuked, be dismissed. For royal authority commands us to show, as the Apostle says: "Honor one another, and let there no longer be impunity among you, provoking each other with insults. Honor yourselves and do not dishonor."

Chapter XL. We immediately command that all children, as is their custom, be restrained from gathering and playing indiscriminately on feast days. For in foolish games, they are incited by a certain demonic impulse, urging each other to impure mixings, learning fornication and the abominable impurity of the Sodomites, theft, and lying, and (drunkenness?), foul language, laziness, and softness. And what more needs to be said about them? Therefore, we command that from now on such gatherings and games be completely prohibited. Moreover, let entertainments be carefully observed, lest any evil and harmful thing arise in their midst. But those found in games, after receiving a warning, shall be dismissed after being beaten with twenty-four lashes.

Chapter XLII. If anyone dying leaves behind great wealth, we absolutely do not want it to be administered outside our authority. For these things must be administered excellently among us, and rather their alms should be piously divided among our brothers in the city. For many receive guardianships, who completely squander the wealth entrusted to them, without any benefit to the soul of the deceased. If it is shown to us that certain individuals, in their last moments, secretly, without our knowledge, have accepted the guardianship of such goods and have squandered them, stripped of all their own possessions, they shall be utterly exterminated. Those who have entered into such guardianships, let them be banished along with the possessions.

Chapter XLIII. Those who have abducted their slaves, or free men from the holy church, to which they have fled, by force, let them be punished with beatings or any other punishment. Upon recognizing them, indeed a slave should be set free; but if he is free and then is taken away and beaten, because of his boldness, as if he were impious, a transgressor and a despiser, and an enemy of God, and dared in the place of Tricanum, where bodies are bought, to be sold for two coins, so that thereafter her shameful face may be covered with disgrace, which she truly dared to take a man similar to himself according to his image away from the hand of the Lord and return it to him.

Chapter XLIV. If anyone out of envy in any art shall have attacked an artisan with injury or slander, or shall have sought to hinder him in his very transactions, let that person receive twelve blows, and let him be burdened with thirty days of work in a public workshop, learning not to harm his brother.

Chapter XLV. A Steward or manager or another delegation, when he performs his office or has done justice to him who has the right, we command that nothing at all be received from him until he has fulfilled his duty, and then let his reward be offered to him, and let it be in accordance with proper justice and not beyond what is due. But those who transgress this, and are found to receive food as if from two sides, let them be degraded in dignity and order, as if raging and brawling gluttons, and thus be brought back to piety.

Chapter XLVI. Whoever, summoned to court according to the law, is justly condemned, shall be taken to the royal workshop, and there shall work for two months, so that he may learn from it to act justly towards his neighbor. If the judgment is different, and the just behavior is accepted, he shall be released. For it is one thing to punish, seize, beat, and defraud anyone unjustly, and another to inquire about unknown matters according to the law.

Chapter XLVII. Because it is necessary for the king to seek the advice of holy men on important matters, and to consult the holy God through them, and thus to accomplish what has seemed better to him. For by acting in this way, he will not be ashamed for eternity.

Chapter XLVIII. The man is the head of the woman. Therefore, even if he is a servant, the man is superior to the woman herself. We forbid, therefore, that he be insulted and despised. A woman who is known to mock men shall have her hair, namely the crown, cut off on the back of her head; and after being publicly rebuked, she shall be dismissed. But if after this she behaves disgracefully and mocks men, after being convicted, the tip of her tongue shall be cut off, and she shall be dismissed. If he raises his hand to strike any man, except the one he fathered, he shall first receive the punishment established for such an offense. But if he does not refrain from such actions and dares to commit them again, showing no regard for our law, his hand shall be cut off. For he dared to raise his own glory against the glory of God, which should belong to man. For the glory belongs to God. If such discipline is necessary for this reason, when there are many servants, let the man correct the men and the women, namely, their female servants. For we command to whip the feet, but we do not command to strike the head.

Chapter XLIX. If a woman desires to marry a second time, let her either enter a monastery recently established by us, if she does not want to be married again, lest Satan tempt her. But if she becomes a widow after a second marriage, even if she does not want to, let her withdraw from the world. For the divine canons prohibit third marriages. The same should be done for men who are left without a spouse.

Chapter L. If those who mix with their fellow servants are found to be sinning together, let one of them lose a breast, and the other the instrument of sin, and then be forgiven.

Chapter LI. If anyone sends his servants on a holiday or on the Lord's day to bring some burden, whether food, wood, wine, excluding drink, which they receive from the suburbs or from the market, excluding delicacies, let the male and female servants be apprehended, and let their burdens be taken from them. But if anyone resists our authority, contradicts, murmurs, and curses, let him be killed by the sword as a witness, so that he may learn to obey the Lord and the laws of the king. Let such a person be exempt from living, knowing how to obey.

Chapter LII. If employers withhold wages from their hired workers, and the worker who suffered the injustice complains that they did not pay him his deserved wages, and they sought to defraud him, let them pay double the price and let the defrauded one receive it.

Chapter LIII. If anyone is found tormenting his slaves by starvation, or cruelly beating them, but not correcting them as a father, after his guilt has been purified and exposed, all his household should be removed from him, and set free as having been wrongfully held in bondage, and they should be sent back to their own families. For it is written that in Christ there is neither slave nor free, but we are all one in him. If a slave seeks only his own advantage and does not obey the just and innocent commands of his master (for there are many who order their slaves to engage in fornication and other wicked deeds), if he does not obey his master in good works, let him be allowed to go free, even if he takes legal action, unpunished.

Chapter LIV. Those who act harshly and cruelly towards their slaves, after their slaves have been freed, shall promise in writing with their own hand that they will no longer purchase other slaves. However, if their worst behaviors are corrected, and they promise not to beat them harshly and inhumanely, the slaves shall be released and not be claimed as free. Besides providing them with double clothing and shoes, their masters shall provide them with other necessary items annually, generously and at their own expense; and if they do not obey their masters as they should, there shall be no one who pities them.

Chapter LV. With all the poor placed in homes for the needy and the elderly, we command that no one should ask for bread in the market square, in churches, or any other place. For my word everywhere proclaims that the hungry, thirsty, and destitute come to us, and in the name of the Lord, they shall receive suitable aid and comfort. For foreign nations that come here complain about us: Christians have no compassion, they say; for their brothers ask for bread, and there is no one to show them mercy. Let us have mercy on our brothers, especially on our teachers and masters.

Chapter LVI. Therefore, whoever is enrolled and in need shall receive without making any demands. If anyone is found demanding, let them be punished with eighteen blows of the stick and confined to the hostel for the elderly, and the prefect of the hostel for the needy shall be warned not to let them leave the hostel thereafter. But if someone is not enrolled, they shall be brought before us, and we shall treat them with mercy. Those who wish to give alms shall go to the hostels for the needy and the elderly and bestow their kindness there. If anyone happens to come across a silent and walking poor person, not begging but seeking help and willing to work, we command that help be given to them.

Chapter LVII. All the buildings of the city, when well-located and greatly increased in value by those who once tyrannically ruled the possessions of the Himyarites, with God's help, we ordered the prices to be lowered. Whoever was paying nine coins, let them pay six, and similarly for all a reduction of one-third. Whoever was paying six, let them pay four, and keep the remaining two for themselves. And so on, let them be counted in a similar manner; give two parts, keep the third; and let no one dare to increase the price of locations in the future. But, as we have established, let them be administered within the same term, without receiving any reduction or increase. But whoever dares to add to the price of the location, or expel tenants with certain gifts, and bring in another in their place, not at a higher price, I say that such a man who has increased the rent at home as if by a gift, [...] first, let all the goods of this person be made public, and let them be expelled from the city as an enemy of their brothers, and ignorant of this precept: What you hate to be done to you by another, see that you do not do to another someday. However, if the master of a certain house truly intends to use it for his own benefit, let him have the freedom to do as he pleases; but for this reason, to educate him, bring in another, with the same established price of the location, and not dare to occupy the entire house. For we do not allow it, unless the tenant is a quarrelsome and disruptive man.

Chapter LVIII. We command every regional prefect to inspect what is happening in the houses in many ways. And if you know of certain crimes committed, report them to the master of that house, and let them be corrected immediately. If they refuse to listen to you, immediately inform us through the magistrate, namely the eparch.

Chapter LIX. Any man should have his female servant as a spouse, so that she can be set free to have as his wife. And provide spouses for the female servants, so that each one has their own comfort and does not sin. But whoever violates this religious command of ours, let the unmarried servant be taken away from him as a punishment, and the maid who does not have a spouse, because he has abolished the kingdom's command and despised the law of the Himyarites. The seized slaves should be handed over to the regional steward, as mentioned earlier, and as we have established it. But if some defend themselves saying, "I am poor and cannot afford to buy a spouse for my servant," we will respond to them: If you are poor, sell your only servant. For we will not tolerate the trading that takes place every day to become licentious because of you.

Chapter LX. Those who wish to live in virginity should not be hindered, and those who wish to preserve chastity should not be obstructed. Let them be required to write with their own hand, so that they do not live in an old-fashioned way, but in secret commit wickedness and sin. However, capital punishment shall be imposed on them based on the written agreement. Let those who can depart, depart. But those who are caught must pay the penalties stated in the written agreement. For we do not want the Pharisees and hypocrites who believe in the Lord Jesus to lie to God and the kings.

Chapter LXI. Any regional prefect who does not observe that royal and God-ordained command with fear, reverence, and prudence, but negligently or accepting bribes, and dares to despise what is written in this command of ours, if found out, we command that he be suspended, with his left foot in chains, led through the middle of the square with his head bowed, on a pole, namely. In any case, the straw should be burned, so that others may be warned by this example. It is expedient that one scabbed goat, separated from the flock, be killed, so that the entire flock may not be contaminated by it. This should be done by the hyparch. But if the hyparch finds the regional prefect violating these instructions, he should be punished. If he has offended him, and does not carry out this most pious and just precept of ours against him, let the hyparch himself suffer, incurring the indignation of our gentleness.

Chapter LXII. Let each prefect inspect the transactions made in his jurisdiction diligently, so that they are done justly. Let them inspect the markets, how goods are sold by merchants; and especially those who sell to them, namely foreign merchants, should be inspected; and thus let goods be sold according to right justice. For often they buy at a high price, often at a low price, often at a moderate price. Let all things be sold in the market at a fair price, so that neither the seller is without profit, nor is the buyer harmed.

Chapter LXIII. We do not permit any linen weaver or weaver, any craftsman of any art, to start even a single hair's work on the holy Sunday. If anyone doing this is caught, we order both his work and his tools to be destroyed by fire in the middle of the market.

Chapter LXIV. Those who do not receive all the household on great feasts and holy Sunday, and those leaving for the holy church together in the evening of Saturday and in the morning of holy Sunday, and in its liturgy and in the evening, let the prefect of the region announce twice before three worthy men that they obey the divine command. But if they do not carry out what is prescribed to them, let all their substance be taken away from them, and let half be divided among the brothers placed in the hospice for the needy. However, let the remaining part be kept for profit by the prefect of this region, along with the soldiers sitting with him, so that they may conduct a more diligent investigation of all those things that we command them.

THE END OF THE LAW

When the blessed Archbishop Gregentius had written all these things in a new volume, he presented it to the most religious King Abram, who ordered them to be read in his presence. And when they were being read, he greatly rejoiced and exulted in spirit. And the king approached and kissed the blessed hands by which they had been written and said: "Blessed be this hour to the Lord, in which it has been said of you: behold, a male child is born." Moreover, the most blessed proposed to the king that these things be transcribed in many other writings, each regional prefect could have their own.

Having done this, the archbishop ordered all the regional prefects to gather in the church. And when the king came with the senate and all the citizens, after the holy offertory was completed, taking the letter, which the most reverend archbishop had written with his own hands, he said to the regional prefects: Come, my beloved, and receive these ordinances from the hand of the Lord, so that, knowing that they were not made by anyone or in any way, but accepted from the Lord Himself, we may hand them over to you. Taking the letters, he read them in front of everyone. After they were read, he ordered that the copied letters be brought and placed on the holy altar. Having done this, he kneeled, prayed, and said: You who see hearts, just, ineffable, fearsome, strong, mighty, holy, Lord, extend your high and holy, strong, fearsome, and great arm, and, receiving these letters placed before your pure eyes, distribute them to your servants as once through Moses you did with the seventy men who had the spirit in them, and as you did with your holy apostles with tongues of fire.

With him praying, a strong wind blew from the Lord, as if from the altar, into the scrolls, and lifting them from the place where they were stored, like leaves carried by the wind through the air, in each region's officials, lifting their folds, he put them down. When this miraculous wonder occurred, all the bystanders with their king and his nobles were filled with fear and awe, and everyone could see them all struck and venerating and magnifying the Lord of hosts with outstretched hands.

The archbishop said to the magistrate: "See, beloved, that from the Lord our God you have received these divine instructions in the form of letters. Therefore, with the fear of God, with trembling, observe so that in this epoch we may be able to enjoy a peaceful and tranquil life. Read all that the Almighty Lord himself has given to us, and in the world to come, let us obtain, for that will not be the end.

This and many other things were said then by the archbishop, and then they all went to their homes, glorifying God. The king, seizing the archbishop's hand, blessed him and brought him to the meal that he had prepared.

We establish this, therefore, after all of the governors of our country, they were given their lot before the eyes of the king, as instituted. This was carried out, in reverence, trembling, and prudence, with what he himself orders and proscribes.

We wish to see honest, purer men, as it is written, purer and more sincere than gold. For they were all walking with fear and trembling, and it was written in the books of the kingdom, executed in haste, albeit reluctantly and unwillingly. So that it was fulfilled by the prophet when he said, in his divine word, "there is no falling off the wall, no crying, no passage into the streets." And afterwards, "Blessed are those", he said, "to whom all things are said. Blessed are those whose God is the Lord.

When this was done, in the hopes that it would succeed, the king sent his praise to the magistrates, telling them not to do anything unjust, and not to let his nobles do as they will. In great joy, they all rejoiced, and the Jews also came up, as they had been asked, for a time of exactly forty days.

They had met there to discuss, and the king did remember all of this, and made preparations for this in the theater (the hall where great royal edicts were kept), this spectacle having been prepared, and all the cohorts having been gathered, etc.

LATIN TEXT

Dei sapientia et intellectus, Sanctus, potens, oculus in pauperem respiciens, palpebra sancla interrogans justum el pium, videant oculi tui semper invigilantes congregatis ante faciem tuam quis sit dignus ad propositum, et fac cum eo signum in bonum, ut et in co glorificetur sanctissimum nomen tuum.

Et cum hæc precatus est, virtus Domini superveniens rapuit in aere dignum, et duxit, el statuit euni coram justo et Elesbaa rege. Videntes autem omnes illud signum admirabile, recesserunt exclamaveruntque attoniti: Kyrie, elison.

Clarissimus vero episcopus respondens, regi dixit : Illud quod tibi ostendit Dominus, piissime, in dextræ tuæ honorem, redde mibi, et pariter crimus in eo, ut Dominus prospere diriget, tuáque, Christi ainans, inansuetudo adjuvabit.

Rex autem, nihil moratus, regiam tunicam confestim porrigens, induit eum, regnique diadema capiti ejus imposuit, et calceamenta in pedes ejus. Cum vero in magnam ecclesiam pervenissent, in sanctæ Trinitatis nomine ædificatam, perfecto diviao sacrificio, particeps quoque processionist ct sancti ad divinum altare introitus juvenis rex una cum piissimo rege Elesbaa factus est.

Quibus rite perfectis, fauste acclamavit exercitus his verbis: "Elesbæ sanctissimi regis Æthiopiæ multi et felices sint anni!" Quod vero septies dixerunt. Deinde acclamaverunt: "Abramii, Christi amantis, Homeritarum regis, optimi el pii, multi sint anni!" Quod, ut juniori regi, decies dictum Et rursus utrique fausta precati suit, dicentes : Elesbæ et Abramii piissimorum regum multi sint anni! Gregentii sanctissimi archiepiscopi nostri el pastoris pacifici, et sani et integri, multi el sancti et boni sint anni!

Quæ cum fausta precatus esset exercitus, reversis in palatio regibus, convivium appositum est, et lautæ dapes exercitui cæterisque magnifice oblatae sunt.

Remansit igitur Elesbaa justissimus, postquam Christi amantem Abramium Homeritarum regem ipse constituit, in illa regione tres et triginta dies, omnia ibi pulchre instituens, sæpiusque recentem regem Abramium admonens, regnum pie regeret, secundum omnia et in omnibus sanctissimo patri Gregentio morem gereret Lecto vero ex exercitu circiter quinque Æthiopum militum millia eis præsidii causa reliquit.

Ipse autem ad Æthiopiam castra movit ; atque co cum incolumis rediisset , gratias agens optimo Deo, neque aurum , neque argentum, neque lapides pretiosos el margaritas ei obtulit; sed et lotum seipsum, hostiam irreprehensibilem, spirilalemque adorationem obtulit Creatori, quo majus non aliud a subjectis suis Deum repetere scimus.

Tradidit igitur regnum suum proprio filio Atherphotham, et pilosa veste induta, in Ophra dictum montem concessit, cœli nebulas prope æmulantem, lit dictum est, atque in deserto situm: ibique seipsum in tenebroso terræ tugurio penitus inclusit, speluncæque occluso aditu, omnes vitæ dies neque cuipiam visus, neque cum ullo conversatus angelicum in modum degit, atque ita ad Dominum purus irreprehensusque pervenit. Escam autem accipiebat quodam foramine ab illlis habitantibus monachis : afferebat eam quidam ex inferiori monte veniens solus, ac deinde revertens.

Inter cætera illud quoque ferunt, esse in hoc monasterio fratrem quemdam juniorem. Qui cum ia ministerium mitteretur, fornicationi ac vino magnopere indulgens, in monasterium deinde revertebatur. Die quadam, eum ea quæ solitus erat fecisset, atque per desertum ad monasterium rediret, prope quædam præcipitia loca ambulantem insolita magnitudine serpens, ex neinore celericursu exsiliens, eum necaturus persequebatur. Ille autem , hinc et illine fugiens, eum fallere nequibat.

Jamque arctius urgebatur, neque quid faceret habebat, serpente ad vorandum eum ingruente, cum ipsius subiit animo beati Elesbaæ cogitatio, respiciensque dixit serpenti : Adjuro te, per sanctissimum et justum Elesbaam regem, recede a me, nee jam me persequere. Serpens vero, reveritus nomen per quod deprecatus erat frater, stetit. Et respondens serpens, humana voce dixieti : Quomodo igitm tibi parcam, cum angelus Domini e cœ mihi, at te comederem, imperaverit, propter impudicitiam et fornicationem tuam, et quia Domini servitio addictus, corpus tuum inquinare non desinis, Spiritumque Dei sanctum exacerbas? Qui vero stans, et audiens, et attonitus quia tanquam homo ipsi loquebatur, contremiscens ut prius rursum adjubatur. Rursus auteni respondens, dixit ei serpens : Fac mibi jusjurandum quod deinceps non immundæ cupiditati indulgebis, qua primus mundo casus fuit, et te incolumem relinquam. Et frater juravit dicens : Per habitantem in cœlis Deum, ac per venerandi sanctique regis Elesbaæ nomen, obtestor me non jam Dominum exacerbaturum, sicut nunc usque male eum exacerbavi fornicans et luxuriose vivens. Factum est autem ut, cum monachi sermonem audiit serpens, prodigium ingens atque mirificum visum fuerit. Ignis enim e cœlo cecidit, serpentemque coram fratre devoravit. Metu autem æ tremore perculsus, pavitans in monasterium suum reversus est, nee jam perseveravit peccare in conspectu Domini, sed vitam finivit in pœnitentia.

Et hæc quidem de co. Beatissimus autem Gregentius, profecto piissimo Elesbaa rege, omnes omnium ecclesiarum presbyteros arcessivit, sapientioribusque ex iis electis, episcopum super urbem ordinavit, jubens simul cum præclarissimo rege Abramio, omnes qui sub corum ditione erant, aut vanam ipsorum religionem reliquerant, baptizari, vel, si perseveraverint, morte plecti.

Promulgato igitur hoc edicto, videre erat onmes cum uxoribus liberisque suis ad divinum regenerationis lavacrum properantes, et per illud ad Christum procedentes. Baptizabant enim omnes episcopi omnes ad eos accedentes per omnem urbem cum pura dispositione: et illuminabatur populus, et multa erant diabolo detrimenta.

Que cum fierent, baptizarenturque multi atque ad veritatis cognitionem ultro venirent, excitati Judæi ex omni regni hujus civitate, atque inter se congressi, concilio adhibito, sibi invicem dixerunt: Quid faciemus nos superstites? Quoniam, nisi baptizemur ut fert regis edictum, interficient nos præfecti ejus, secundum imperium quod ab co edixerunt. Et cum consilii ancipites essent, alii quidem dicebant: Faciamus voluntatem regis, ne immature moriamur, atque in abscondito rur-sus fidem nostram colamus. Alii autem dicebant: Verum, si hoc fecerimus, nonne videt Deus legem suam a nobis violari? Et ipse cum Deus sit ultiolum, retributionem, nobis reddet, et omnes magis peribimus. Alii dicebant: Nunc jam non nobis Deo opus est, quoniam pium regem nostrum Du-naanum Elesha manibus tradidit interficiendum eam exercitu ejus. Propere igitur, si vobis placet, cuncta nostra furtim auferentes, illico hanc regionem digrediamur, ne cum corporibus animas quoque perdamus. Dixerunt et alii: Quod si migrare vo'umushocmodo quem dixistis; et hæc no-verint Christiani, quæ in nos sint exercituri mala plane vobis compertum est.

Unus vero ex eis, llerbanus nomine, vir legis doctor, disertus atque astutissimus, Veterisque Testamenti peritissimus, cæteræque disciplinæ non rudis, respondens dixit eis Vos omnes vana quædam excogitavistis, nihilque quod vobis expediat in medium protulistis. Quod si igitur mihi vultis assentiri, protinus a rege et Gregentio episcopo postulabimus nonnullos eligat viros nobiscum disputare volentes, ut, si quidem nos vi sermonum persuaserint, ex animi sententia Christiani flamus; si vero non persuadeant, manifestum sit eos nobis vim inferre, ut a fide nostra deficiamus. Quare noverimus et nos qualis sit eorum fides. Si enim vera est, credemus (scimusne annon forte jam venerit Messias, et non ignoraverimus); si autem falsa inventa est, sciemus nos propter Deum mori, mortemque acriter complectemur.

Quæ cum ille dixisset, tumultuantur onines, Heranoque dicunt: Videmus te quoque Christians avere. Veramne fidem nostram esse nescis? et quomodo cam relinquemus? Dixit Herbanus: Nihil, fratres, malum dixi. Scitote enim nos qua ibet ratione baptizari coactum iri. Si igitur mihi on creditis, nulli vestrum male consului. Denique, si fidem eorum non experti eritis, et sine experimento credideritis, sicut isti jusserunt feceritis; i autem non credideritis, neminem vestrum fugit nos ab iis interfectum iri, et moriemur. Et his Herbani dictis assensi sunt.

Omnes igitur in libello omnia argumenta sua conscripserant, dederuntque regi. Rexautem, aperto lectoque quem porrexerant libello, adeo iratus est ut eos vellet interficere. Attamen paulum mitescens, arcessivit archiepiscopum, libellumque ei tradidit. Quo lecto, rem optime se habere censuit beatus vir, regique dixit: Recte aiunt Judæi ex animi sententia quam vi credere potius esse. Sine eos nunc disputare ut expetunt, et cum persuaserimus eos, si baptizari recusant, tunc plecte eos, sicut jubet tuum in Christo regnum. Quibus auditis, rex dedit eis quadraginta dierum dilationem, ut eo tempore deliberarent, et quos vellent eligentes, ad seipsum ad disputandum mitterent.

Qui igitur profecti sunt, atque in omnibus eorum regionibus quæsierunt homines qui convenirent, ac deinde coram rege irent ad disputandum. Expleto igitur præfixo tempore, beatissimus Gregentius hæc consilia dedit justo et piissimo regi, ut commuhi bono consuleret, et ordines pie ordinaret.

Jube, inquit, o rex, secundum honestam electionem cuique regioni ducem constitui, in primis regiæ Homeritarum civitati, et sic deinde cæteris om-mibus tui regni civitatibus ex proceribus eorum. Curaque hec constituta erunt, func quæ ipsis sint cavenda scriptura statuamus.

Rex igitur, adnumeratis una et triginta regionibus, atque in primis regia urbe Negra, statim cuique regioni præfectos imposuit, numero, ut dictum est, unum et triginta, jussitque unumquemque ex iis proprium habere suggestum in regione quam sortitus erat, in medio foro; inscriptasque domos omnes, in quibus imperium exercent, habere eos jussit, ut ditionis suæ limites cognoscerent, neque erraret alius in aliam ditionem inspiciens atque ordinans. Atque his ita constitutis, statuens officiales, tribuit eis imperium super sexdecim milites. Et cum hæc comparasset, jussit rex accipere stipendia, et largitias, et annonas, et agere recle cum prudentia ac Dei timore. Imperavit etiam beatissimo Gregentio ut perscriptam ordinationem faceret eisque præberet, qua diligenter scirent quæ sibi essent cavenda.

Hæc meditatus sedato animo beatus, quæ sibi imperata erant exsequi cœpit.

Rex autem senum, et ægrotantium, et egenorum, et peregrinorum hospitia celerrime fecit, multa in eis thesanrizans. Namque ex redditibus magnorum horum suburbiorum, quæ condiderat Dunaanus Hebræorum rex et proceres ejus, omnes egenos, atque in inopia senes et infirmos, claudosque et cæcos, magnificentissime curavit et refecit, stipendia per totum annum præbens eis, et vestimenta, et cibum, et vinum, et oleum, et fructus, et omne genus bonorum, ita ut famam et laudem sibi compararet. Patriarcham enim Abrahamum alterum vocabant, regenique Job alterum, propter hospitalem ejus animum, infinitamque beneficentiam. Nam sanctorum memorias cum celebraret, duas mensas apponi jubebat, egenorum unam, alteram ipsius proceribus. Cœnæ autem hora, egenorum mensæ semper accumbens comedebat, et unicuique magnificentissima dona largiebatur. Si quis ab eo aliquid boni expostularet, statim exaudiebat, et non invito animo dabat. Adeo ut eo regnante nemo pauper ejus in regno inveniretur, neque inique agens, sicut scriptum est, neque patiens injuriam. Frenavitque Deus omnem populum a circuitu ejus. Et in diebus ejus bellum non exortum est, sed pax profunda, lætitia, et charitas, et sedula pauperum cura, et viduarum orphanorumque præsidium, et justitiæ ineffabilis, et festorum spiritalium, et ecclesiarum mirum in modum constitutio.

Venerandam autem legem, quam sanctus Gregentius quasi ab ipso rege condidit, huic narrationi adjicere decrevi. Ilis verbis edicta est:

Cum Redemptor noster atque omnipotens Deus, per ineffabilem benignitatem multumque in homines amorem nostræ utilitati consulens, suscitavit nos ad hoc excelsum clarissimæ et summæ potestatis fastigium, decet nos benefactori gratias agere, et juxta vires, amorem potestatemque nostram ei servire. Neque enim ob dignitatem et gloriam (quid igitur nobis unquam dehere poterat?) benigne nos excitavit, præclarissimum Homeritarum imperium nobis largiens, verum ut profecto, sinceris ejus mandatis dociles, cum metu, et tremore, et alacritate nobis ab eo præcepta celeriter perageremus, nobismetipsis, ut opinor, tali incepto optime facientes, non tantum in præsenti, sed et in futuro tempore. Etenim cum manifestavit Deus Mosi mandata ejus et præcepta tempore exitus ejus ex Ægypto, hæc de populo dixit ad eum : Si auditu audieris vocem Domini Dei tui, et quod rectum est coram co feceris, cunctum languorem, quem posui in Ægypto, non inducam super te. Quapropter igitur, ne et ipsi, sicut Ægyptii, justas ejus minas experiamur, mandata ejus cum timore servemus.

INITIUM LEGIS.

Cap. I. Igitur jubet mansuetudo nostræ pietatis ad eos qui imperium in vicinos hujusce regiæ urbis urbes acceperunt cum tremenda auctoritate, eas, præsertimque hanc urbem urbium caput, quam maximo ordine componi, atque utinam ita fiat in omnem ditionis nostræ civitatem. Jubemus autem ut subditi potentiæ nostræ, si diligentes sint, revereantur sedentes vos eo quo par est apparatu in publicis quæ mansuetudo mea tribuit locis. Inspicite igitur secure communia loca, plateas urbis, vias, cenopolia, domos, venalia ommia, panem scilicet, et vinum, et quodvis obsonium. Et quisque regionem, quam sortitus est, fideliter servet. Alium enim in proximi ejus administrationem et gubernationem non inspicere jubemus, sed quemque quæ sua sunt regere volumus.

Cap. II. Cavendum est igitur ne fiat cædes. Si qua fieret, comprehensum occisorem protinus majori potentiæ tradentes, in prætorium deducite. Inspicite ne fiat adulterium, incestus, bestialitas. Si qui unquam tale scelus admiserint, ad prætorium eos deducite.

Cap. III. Inspicite ne fiat turpis Sodomitarum libido. Si quis vero deprehensus fuerit, comprehensum ad magistratum deducite, ut ille secundum Domini legem sæviat in eos. Æquum est enim eos interfici, ne viventes fetore peccati et abominationis eorum, ut ita dicam, inquinent et alias animas immaculatas innocentium hominum, et iram Dei in nos immunditiis suis incitent.

Cap. IV. - Inspicite ne sit magia, aut veneficium, aut incantatio. At, si quis unquam deprehendatur, statim hæc faciens ad prætorium tradatur, ut igne tale scelus admissi comburantur. Inspicite ne sint præstigi, aut falsum testimonium. Si quis forte talia auderet, tradatur iste magistratui, et linguæ primoris acumen ei præcidatur.

Cap. V. Invigilate vigilantia multa, et sedulo attendite furibus et illis qui eorum furta accipiunt aut celant. Primum eos quinquaginta fustium verberibus multate; deinde signo aliquo, nempe sigillo ferreo ardente frontem eorum signantes, sic coram populo tunica nudatum dimittite eum, dicentes eis Cavete vobïs, fratres: a furto deinceps abstinete, ne comprehensi majore pæna afliciamini. Si postea quivis denuo in simili facinore deprehendatur (quod manifestum faciet sigillum in fonte impressum), ad magistratum adducatur, et abscisso pedis dextri nervo eum dimittite, ut, si furari voluerit, inerti permanente pede ejus, deambulare nequeat. Ac deinde in pauperum hospitio nostri regni collocetur, ut inde deinceps quotidianum cibum accipiat.

Cap. VI. Omnem virum, omnemque mulierem fugere immundam fornicationem jubemus. Vir quis- que propriam habeat uxorem, et ne sit eis speciosa defensio quod multi dicunt: Semper sum pauper et uxorem habere non possum. Quibus contra respondemus : Non vis te legitimo matrimonio conjungere, neque nos cogimus. Cave autem ne cum pellicibus peccans inveniaris, ac protinus pericliteris. Jubet enim nostri regni mansuetudo quemvis in fornicatione deprehensum, sive masculum, sive feminam, centum fustium flagellorum ictus accipere; ac deinde istius auris dextra præcidatur : denique publicationem passus dimittatur. Pariter et quævis mulier, quae virum non habet, con prehensa simili afficiatur pœna. Si autem deprehensus fuerit vir uxorem non habens cum muliere proprium virum non habente, ac velint deinceps legi. timo conjungi matrimonio, et placide sapienterque vivere, advocato sacerdote, ab iis qui eos deprehen. derunt, benedicti dimittantur.

Cap. VII. Si quis cum muliere in viri potestate fuerit inventus, statim ei corporis membrum, cum quo peccatum committit, abscidatur; sinistra quoque mulieris mamma, cum qua proprium deseruit virum et cum Satana commiscuit. Expedit enim, dixit Dominus, ut pereat unum membrorum tuorum, quam totum corpus tuam mittatur in geben. næ ignem.

Cap. VIII. Quicunque legitime uxorem habens, et ea relicta cum alia fornicatur, parte qua peccatum fecit præcidatur. Si autem ejus conjux reperta sit dicens: Non id peccato viro meo tribuo et si sexcenties mihi fraudem fecerit : sed virum meum impunitam volo. Accipiat vir talis ducenta flagrorum verbera, et sinistra aure abscissa, post publicationem, uxori suæ reddatur.

Cap. IX. Idem et de muliere adulterante. Pro mamma, auris abscidatur, si viro ejus placet cum ea cohabitare. Si autem post hæc eadem patrantes deprehensi fuerint, priorem pœnam subeant, huic quidem mamma, illi autem virilia resecenter. Ac deinde si rursus talia committens mulier deprehensa fuerit, calcis ictibus afflicta talis femina ex urbe ejiciatur.

Cap. X. Si viri divitis Blius pauperem puellam adamaverit, nolintque ejus parentes, eo quod pauperem non miserati sunt atque respuerunt, lex eos connubio jungat, constituta a parentibus filio suo dote integra, sicut regium jussum imperat. Idem quoque de divite puella pauperis juvenis amore capta.

Cap. XI. Sequatur vir liber, si fit matrimonium, et domino vel domina ancillæ famuletur

Idem quoque fiat de libera muliere, cum se servo incongruenter submiserit. Tollens enim membra Christi, et faciens membra meretricis, dignus est qui hominis famulus flat, ut quantum malum sit peccatum noverit.

Cap. XII. Quemque jubemus propriam unicamque uxorem habere, abominandamque fornicationem fugere, propter quam venit ira Dei e eœlis super filios hominum. Qui hæc transgreditur manifeste audiit quas debeat poenas persolvere.

Cap. XIII. Jubet nostra a Deo regalis auctoritas a parentibus suis liberos a decem usque ad duodecim annos matrimonio conjungi, præter infirmitatis casum. Hujus vero legis violator præbeat, si quidem est locuples, sex aur: libras regionis suæ præfecto; si autem mediocris, tres; si vero minoris census, unam et dimidiani; si et inferioris, libram unam; qui autem post eum, sex et triginta nummos; post hunc, decem et octo; deinde novem; deinde quatuor et dimidium; deinde duos et trientem; deinde unum et sextam partem, et deinde dimidium. Tunoque isti vocationem non exspectent, sed ocius quæ jussi sunt persolvant. Qui moram fecerit, regio decreto ex urbe exterminetur.

Cap. XIV. Quemque jubemus divina pacificæ majestatis nostræ mandata violantem, secundum facultates suas, ut præscriptum est, plecti. Quæ ab eo repelentur percipiat ipsius regionis præfectus, cum militibus sibi assidentibus.

Cap. XV. Si quis animadverterit proximum suum in pravo atque iniquo negotio versantem, neque hujus admonuerit regionis suæ præfectum, ac fuerit deprehensus, si quidem locuples, duo et septuaginta flagrorum verbera coram populo acciiat; si vero pauper, quatuor nummis aureis ; si minoris census, tribus; si inferioris adhuc conditionis, duobus ; et si omnino inops, uno nummo inultetur.

Cap. XVI. Si quis fuerit adulteriorum internuntius, vel conciliaverit impurissimum complexum puerorum vel eunuchorum, quibuscum iniquitatem facere solent stulti, et amentes, et impii, sive vir, sive mulier, sive qualiscunque sit persona, atque deprehensus fuerit iste talia faciens, jubemus huic linguam a dimidio resecari, ut, si deinceps voluerit Satanæ famulari, sicut serpens olim in paradiso, per linguam suam, minime possit. Maledicti enim sunt iniqui isti, quod vanis labiorum suorum loquelis hominem quasi dementant, eumque diabolo in animæ perniciem tradunt.

Cap. XVII. Qui domos suas fornicationis diversoria faciunt, atque in eis iniquitatem agentes excipiunt proteguntque, quotquot in eo deprehensi fuerint, adducantur apud magistratum cum omni substantia, et ejiciantur ex urbe, manu scripla promissione se non jam eadem facturos esse, omnesque vitæ suæ dies procul a publicis rebus victuros. Dæmonum enim ministros mansuetudo nostra in urbibus ditioni nostræ subjectis versari non sinit. Quemadmodum enim jampridem persecutus est pessimus diabolus per reges idololatria furentes dilectos et cultores Domini nostri Jesu Christi, sustulit vero et immaculatam fidem nostram a facie Christianorum e terra, sic pariter visum est nostræ ex Deo potestati tollere omnes pompas draconis istius, qui cecidit a cœlis a facic terræ nostre, el pro facultate nostra omnem ejus malitiam nequitiamque per credentes in Christum persequi.

Cap. XVIII. Nos autem jusjurandum quod juravit Deus ad Abraham patrem nostrum explentes, statuimus quod non cessabimus omnes vitæ nostræ dies innumerabilia mala conferentes omnibus qui operantur iniquitatem, nostramque hanc a Deo datam legem pedibus conculcant, nisi peccatum facere desierint. Sin aliter, disperdere eos non prætermittemus. Etenim mirabilis David, similia his perficiens, mundo respondebat: In matutino interficiebam omnes peccatores terræ ut disperderem de civitate Domini omnes operantes iniquitatem.

Cap. XIX. Qui in itinere mulieres adoriuntur, eisque vim inferunt, sicut latrones Deique inimici, convicti ab ipsa muliere cum juramento, circiter centum fustium verbera accipiant, et utraque aure abscissa, dimittantur. Et si post hæc eadem facientes deprehendantur, ducenta flagra passi ejiciantur.

Cap. XX. Si qui per agoram sive plateam iter facientes, manus injiciant turpiter in transeuntes feminas, bacchicæ et inhoneste concupiscentiæ causa, quibusdam spectantibus, muliere vero exclamante, multetur vir talis duobus et septuaginta fustium verberibus in media agora coram populo, et publicatus, admonitione accepta, dimittatur. Si autem rursus deprehensus fuerit eadem faciens, manus ei, tanquara impudentissimo, abscidatur. Nostra enim mansuetudo jussit quemquam habere propriam consortem, in aliam vero manum non injicere, nec, si fieri potest, oculo innuere.

Cap. XXI. Christianos enim fornicatores, vel adulteros, vel sodomitas, vel magos et incantatores, vel similia bis facientes, regale nostrum imperium in regno versari non sinit. Quapropter enim misit Deus a cœlo iram suam in nos, ad conterendum atque delendum nos in fiuem. Ideo neque in itineribus bellorum prospere cedimus propter peccata ista : arma enim, ait, belli justitia; et si populus meus audisset me, Israel si in viis meis ambulasset, pro nibilo forsitan inimicos eorum humiliassem, et super tribulantes eos misissem manum meam, dicit Deus. Itaque omnis nequitia et iniquitas tollatur e medio nostri, et colatur omnis virtus omnisque justitia et veritas, ut et gentes, quæ nos circumdant, nobis subjiciat Dominus Deus noster.

Cap. XXII. Homini a Domino ficto seipsum in omni actione defendere non jubemus, nisi prius acceperit tutelam juxta legem, interrogatus de lege, sicut lex præcipit. Qui vero illud ab hoc die ausi fuerint, etsi sit e proceribus, sive dives aliquis aut pauper, sive delator, sive apparitor, sive nostri sodalitii, aut miles, aut quivis alius nostræ auctoritati subditorum, scilicet verberare, aut colapho cædere, aut calce ferire, aut fuste vel flagris plectere quemvis, sive juste, sive injuste, sine legis arbitrio, sive in foro, sive in via, sive in domo.

Exceptis doctrinas et artes docentibus cum litteris, nec non si herus servum suum, paterve filium et filiam : et hi quidem, justam ob causam; neque, ut quidam ad irascendum proni, docere volentes, occidant hominem. Et nos a talia docentibus jubemus urbice regionis præfectos reposcere syngraphas manu propria scriptas, qua spondeant se non docturos. Si igitur imperium nostrum transgredientes et adulterantes, et vi simplices mediocrisque sortis homines flagellantes aut verberantes deprehensi fuerint, accipiant ad sex et triginta fustium verbera; unusque huic abscidatur pedis digitus; et publice admoniti dimittantur, ut ex iis noscant quantum dolorem afferat colaphus unus, una fustigatio, quemadmodum iste passus est de solo corporis ipsius digito. Nostra enim regia auctoritas oves esse omnes exoptat Christi et Dei, non contendentes, non clamitantes, non autem veneniferas bestias, quæ aliæ alias devorant.

Cap. XXIII. Non licet tibi hominem tui similein verberare. Ne verbera igitur, ne eas in indignationem. Homo es alicujus e proceribus; ne ob præclaram domini tui dignitatem confisus, inopis capiti ictum impingas. Sisne sodalitii nostri, an delator, ne percutias eum, nisi lex jusserit. Dives es et injuriam passus es : confuge ad legem et exinde ultionem accipe. Potens es: bene fac, non autem male. Inops es : parem tui inopem ne pereutias. Injuriam es passus coram judicibus cita; et si non conciliatus fueris, ad nos deveni, et inveniemus in quem occurreris; atque ita confirmabo judicium tuum, si jus tibi est.

Cap. XXIV. Viro non licitum facimus propriam verberare conjugem. Fornicatores enim domum superveniunt media nocte, et criminante tarditatem muliere, ejus opprobrium non ferentes, verberare incipiunt. Si et femina fornicatur, neque etiam virum eam verberare permittimus; sed scripto libello eam judici denuntiet. Quæ autem in peccato suo inventa est, adulterarum mulierum, pœnas juxta legem luat. Si quis autem inventus fuerit regiæ auctoritatis nostræ præceptum violans, siquidem focuples fuerit, sex et triginta fustium plagas accipiat, acceptaque admonitione dimitta. tur; si autem inops, secundum ipsius facultatem multetur. Quod si post hæc eadem quoque ausi sint, adducantur, quasi regii præcepti violatores, atque bona eorum, si quidem sint inferiora, regionis præfectus cum militibus ipsum sequentibus dividat; si vero magna et superiora, regio dispensatori tradat. Ili autem e civitate exterminentur.

Cap. XXV. Hominem vero nimia ebrietate madentem, sive mulierem, et per forum iter facientem, vacillantemque pedibus, et muros subinde conterentem, comprehendi jubemus, includique et usque ad posterum mane retineri. Et cum istius discussa fuerit ebrietas, tinc educatur et sexaginta plagas accipiat; triginta vero, si femina fuerit; admonitusque dimittatur. Scriptum est enim quod Ebriosi regnum Dei non possidebunt.

Cap. XXVI. Observentur autem Jumenta sua vel seipsos gravibus et ægre tolerabilibus oneribus onerantes. Tales comprehendantur, acceptisque sex et triginta verberibus, dimittantur admoniti. Robustus enim mulus duodecim metretas ferat; inferior autem decem; asellus vero octo; quod si et infirmior, sex. Hoc igitur modo onera accipiant. Scriptum est enim: Miseretur justus juinentorum suorum animas; viscera autem impiorum crudelia.

Cap. XXVII. Die festi Dominici, seu sanctæ Dominicæ, jubemus nihil aliud vendi nisi quæ ad hominum jumentorumve escam prosunt; reliqua autem omittantur. Cujus præcepti transgressor, quæcunque proposuerit, præter cibaria sicut modo præscriptum est, amittat, et ipse ejiciatur. Quod vero emptum fuerit, sive jumentum, sive bos, sive ovis, sive aliud adhuc viventium et magnorum animalium, præter ea quae in macello occiduntur, et aves que venduntur, sive vestis, sive quodvis aliud, cibariis exceptis, hæc omnia regionis præfecto, circumstantibusque eum militibus permittantur.

Cap. XXVIII. Die magni festi, aut ipsius sancte et Christianæ Dominicæ, si quis onus vehit, præter cibaria, demigrantesque in longinquam regionem, sive per navigium, sive per seipsum, sive per jumentum, adducatur onus, si est, et jumentum cum onere; atque sic vapulatus ejiciatur quod, cum Christianus sit, haud secus ac Judæus festum ipsius contempsit.

Cap. XXIX. Non vult igitur nostra divinitas quemquam vendere, vel onus ferre, vel fodere, vel laborare, vel quidquam facere in sancta, Dominica, aut in solemnibus magnisque Domini festis, aut vectigalia colligere, vel in festis Deiparæ, aut duodecim sanctorum apostolorum Dei nostri et Christi et Salvatoris, aut reliquorum sanctorum. Hæc vero ad arbitrium nostrum remitto. Transgressores autem, allatis rebus venditisque spoliati, acceptis circiter quatuor et viginti plagis, remittantur.

Cap. XXX. Qui propter magistratuum aut regis præsentiam in obsoniis pretii legitimi et necessarii dimidium jaciunt, vendentibus pauperibus negotiatoribus vi facta, et quæ sunt illorum rapiunt, atque iter facientes, illos auxilio suo vocantes vapulantur, cum hæc agentes deprehensi fuerint, circiter duodecim fustium verbera accipiant. et publice admoniti dimittantur. Regia enim auctoritas nostra fraudatores, et injustos, et raptores ministros habere non patitur. Placet tibi aliquid : præbe justum pretium, aufer illud, et perge viam.

Cap. XXXI.Legem igitur ferimus: Quicunque deprehensus fuerit in tali protervia, edoctus et publice monitus, et post hæc, talibus semel usus, si rursus captus fuerit talis, in publica nostri regni officina hune virum includi jubemus, atque ibi quatuer menses solidos cum opificibus laborare. Sicut enim stulte ac violenter aggressus est, sic docendus est. Atque ita dimittatur, quanto labore panem suum consequantur pauperes ipse expertus.

Cap. XXXII. Qui per regionem nostram certamen faciunt, quique in foro, comprehendantur omnes et ad quadraginta plagas accipiant, propterea quod inordinate violentas manus inter se inferre ausi sunt, aut fustem, aut alio quovis modo. Si autem pars una, legem reverita, cessit, manusque non extulit ad defendendum, et spoliata fuit ab adversario et quodam modo verberata, ille quidem tanquam innocens dimittatur; qui autem illum adortus est, quisquis sit, octoginta plagas accipiat, dein duobus mensibus in nostri regni publica officina inclusus laboret, et postea dimittatur.

Cap. XXXIII. Jumenta ducentes sive onerata sive exsoluta, vel pecus aliud, si videntur irati ea crudeliter verberare, comprehensi vice sua triginta fustium verbera accipiant; nempe dolore suo intelligent quam sit acerbum vapulari. Etenim jumenta quoque, etsi non conversantur neque loquuntur, pariter ac nos vapulati dolore afficiuntur. Manifestum quippe ex iis istos, cum non propria jumenta miscrentur, sic pariter neque hominem miseraturos esse.

Cap. XXXIV. Qui pellinas personas impudenter induunt, atque per vias urbis lascivientes bacchantesque, quasi Satanae turpem ditionem amplexi, et Christiani nomen delentes, necnon jusjurandum illud: Renuntio Satanæ omnique pompa cjus, palam retractantes, ducentas plagas accipant, ignique injiciatur eorum sive capillus, sive barba, et publice admoniti tales viri, in regiam officinam abducantur, annumque totum labori incumbant, servi sint an liberi, ut sciant deinceps in pietate ac Dei timore incedere, neque, idololatrarum operum participes, animas suas ipsi pessumdent.

Cap. XXXV. Citharœdi, et lyristæ, et tragœdi, et crepitacula digitis pulsantes, saltatoresque multentur, viri sint an mulieres, puellæ an adolescentuli. Namque in diebus nostræ pietatis nostrique regni talia patrari non sustinemus, neque ab obvio quovis. In omni enim urbe et regione ditioni nostræ subjecta, neque citharœdum esse vo lumus, neque lyristen, neque tragoedum ant saltatorem, sive virum, sive mulierem, sive adolescentulum, sive adolescentulam, neque parvum, neque magnum. Omnes autem cupimus esse bonos piosque, et Dominum timentes. Qui autem lætari vult quod æquo animo est, psallat. Sed nescio, ait, psallere. Pravi dæmonis didicisti carmina, nullo in libro scripta; Dei vero psalmodiam perscriptam non didicis !

Cap. XXXVI. Tragœdum omnem, et crepitacula digitis pulsantem, et saltatorem, atque omne impuri turpisque ludi genus in regni nostri terra versari nolumus. Transgressores comprehendantur, et fustigentur, et flammis, id est, fumigatione afficiantur et publice objurgati, ad totius anni laborem in regia officina damnentur.

Cap. XXXVII. Idem patiantur qui tesseris ludunt, qui tribolim lascivasque saltationes agunt, et qui eas fingunt, [...] omnes jactatum non præcipimus, nisi quidem ad modestiam sæpius quorumdam mente et manu agitata, sicut triadium et fere similia.

Cap. XXXVIII. Præcipimus iis qui exaltari volunt, spiritualiter ad hoc tendere in sanctis ecclesiis, neinpe per orationem, per lectiones, per psalmodias et per eleemosynam. In quibus omnes lætari oportet, tanquam vere Christianos, tanquam servos Christi, tanquam filios lucis, tanquam regni cœlorum hæredes, precantes ex domo Domini exire, ad Dei domum orantes exsultantesque accedere, se invicem diligere, et virtutibus sicut sol, fulgere.

Cap. XXXIX. Qui injuriis opprobriisque se invicem lacessunt, capti, quatuor et viginti fustium verberibus acceptis, dimittantur, sive masculi sint, sive feminæ. Quod si quis in alium opprobrium conjicit et quasi jaculatur, hic vero, propter præcepti nostri timorem, non quidquam respondens, ad magistratum potius confugit, accipiat qui injuriam intulit octo et quadraginta plagas, et publice objurgatus dimittatur. Jubet enim regia auctoritas mostra, sicut dicit Apostolus: Honore invicem prævenientes, nec jam inter vos impunitum esse, sese invicem opprobriis lacessere. Honorificate enim vosmetipsos et non inhonorate.

Cap. XL. Pueros omnes, sicut mos est eis, incondite in festorum diebus convenire et collu- dere, protinus jubemus inhiberi. Commisti enim insipientibus ludis dæmoniaco quodam impulsu, ad impuras mistiones se invicem hortantur, fornicationem discentes et abominatam Sodomilarum impuritatem, furtum, et mendacium, et minen (ebrietatem?), turpiloquium, et ignaviam, et mollitiem. Et quid plura dicere de iis opus est? Ideo jubemus ut in posterum istius modi conventus et ludi omnino prohibeantur. Cæterum et oblectationes omnes diligenter observentur, ne forte in medio earum quidquam malum et noxium exoriatur. Qui autem in ludis inventi fuerint, quatuor et viginti loris cæsi, admonitione accepta dimittantur.

Cap. XLII. Si qui morientes magna bona reliquerint, extra nostram auctoritatem administrari ea prorsus nolumus. Oportet enim apud nos hæ optime administrari, et potius eleemosynas eorum obæratis in civitate fratribus nostris pie dividi. Multi enim tutelas accipiunt, qui creditas sibi opes penitus decoquent, sine ulla defuncti animæ utilitate. Si nobis ostensum fuerit quod quidam in extremis clam, nobis insciis, tales bonorum tutelas acceperunt, eaque profuderunt, omnibus propriis facultatibus nudati, ipsi denique exterminentur.

Cap. XLIII. Qui servos suos, vel liberos homines e sancta ecclesia, in quam confugerunt, vi abductos, verberibus vel alio quovis supplicio afficiunt, agnitis illis, servus quidem in libertatem vindicetur; si vero liber est qui exinde abstractus et vapulavit, propter audaciam, quasi impius, transgressorque et contemptor, et Dei inimicus, qui talia ausus est in Tricano loco, ubi corpora emuntur, duobus vendatur monetis, ut exinde pudore suffundatur inhonestatum os ejus, quod prorsus ausus est e Domini manu similem ipsius secundum imaginem hominem abstrahere eique reddere.

Cap. XLIV. Si quis ob invidiam in omni arte artificem injuria vel calumnia lacessiverit, vel in ipsis negotiationibus ei obsistere quæsierit, duodecim plagas accipiat iste, et triginta dies in publica officina laborando gravetur, fratri non invidere discens.

Cap. XLV. - Dispensatorem aut mandatorem aut delegationem aliam consecutum, cum fungitur officio aut debitam ei qui jus habet justitiam fecit, jubemus nihil prorsus ab eo accipere dum munus suum expleverit, et tune offeratur ei merces sua, eaque juxta decentem justitiam et non ultra debilum. Qui vero illud transgressi fuerint, inventique tanquam a duobus partibus victum accipientes, dignitate atque ordine detrudantur, quasi furentes helluonesque vapulantes, atque ita ad pietatem reducantur.

Cap. XLVI. Quicunque in jus vocatus, juxta legem juste damnatus fuerit, in regiam officinam ducatur, ibique duos menses labore exerceatur, ut exinde erga proximum suum jam non injuste agere discat. Si aliter sententia tulerit, justusque habitus jus suum acceperit, absolutus dimittatur. Namque aliud est quemvis injuria multare, arripere, verberare et defraudare, et aliud de ignotis rebus legem interrogare.

Cap. XL.VII. Quia oportet regem de magnis rebus sanctorum virorum adhibere consilium, atque per eosdem sanctum Deum interrogare, atque ita quæ ei visa fuerunt melius perfici. Sic enim agens in æternum non confundetur.

Cap. XLVIII. Vir mulieris caput. Masculus igitur, etsi sit famulus, ipsa muliere potior est. Prohibemus igitur ne hunc contumelia afficiat et contemnat. Femina quæ mares irridere cognita fuerit, resecentur crines, nempe cæsaries, in aversa capitis parte; atque eadem publice objurgata dimittatur. Quod si post hæc turpiter sese habuerit maresque irriserit, postquam fuerit convicta, resecetur extrema lingua dementi, et dimittatur. Si manum sustulerit ad quemvis marem percutiendum, præter quem genuit, prius de contumelia constitutam pœnam accipiat. Quod si exinde non se a talibus abstinuerit, sed eadem rursus patrare ausa fuerit, legem nostram nihilo æstimans, abscidatur manus ejus, quod, cum hominis gloria esse debeat, ausa sit suam gloriam adversus gloriam Dei tollere. Gloria enim Dei vir. Quod si disciplina causa hæc necessaria fuerint, cum multi sunt famuli, vir quidem viros corrigat mulier autem mulieres, ancillas scilicet suas. Pedes enim nos jubemus verberare, caput minime præcipimus.

Cap. XLIX. Mulier vi lua ad secundum matrimonium convolet; vel in monasteriis a nobis nuper institutis se recipiat, si altero matrimonio conjungi nolit, ne forte tentet eam Satanas. Si vero post alterum matrimonium viduatur, etiamsi nolit, de mundo secedat. Divini enim canones tertias nuptias prohibent. Idem quoque de viris conjuge orbatis fiat.

Cap. L. Qui cum suis commatribus miscentur, si simul in peccato sint deprehensi, huic quidem nammam, illi vero peccati instrumentum statim abscidatur, ac deinde remittantur.

Cap. LI. Si qui famulos suos in die magni festi, aut in sancta Dominica, latum mittunt onus quoddam, sive pabulum, sive ligna, sive vinum, potu excepto, que veniunt ipsis a suburbio, sive ex venditione, exceptis obsoniis, comprehendantur famuli necnon famula, atque onera sua ab eis auferantur. Si quis vero auctoritati nostræ resistat, atque contradicit, et mussitat, et exsecratur, re teste, gladio is occidatur, ut discat parere Domino regiisque institutis.

Cap. LII. Qui mercenarii mercedem detinent, criminante eo qui injuriam passus est, quia meritam ei mercedem non dederunt, ea vero illum spoliare quæsierunt, duplex pretium solvant, accipiat. que qui fraudatus est.

Cap. LIII. Si quis inventus fuerit fame famulos suos excrucians, aut crudeliter verberans, non autem paterna castigatione, purificata ejus culpa et manifestata, auferantur ab isto omnes domestici, atque in libertatem vindicati remittantur, expostlatis etiam ipsorum conjugibus apud dominos suos. Scriptum est enim quod in Christo non est servus, neque liber, omnes autem unum sumus salvati in eo. Si propriam utilitatem omnino quærit servus, nec domini sui præceptis paret justis atque innoxiis (sunt enim multi qui servos suos sibi præstare operam jubent in fornicatione atque in aliis pravis operibus); non obediens domino suo in opere bono, sinatur, etiamsi in jus vocat, inultus.

Cap. LIV. Qui sæve et atrociter erga famulos suos sese habent, in libertatem vindicatis servis eoruin, syngraphis sua manu scriptis spondeant se non jam alios empturos esse servos. Si autem emendantur pessimi mores, pollicenturque non jam eos sæve et inhumaniter verberare, remittantur servi neque in libertatem vindicentur. Præbeant autem eis, præter duplicem vestem et calceos, et cætera necessaria quotannis domini eorum, opulenter et sumptum præbentes eis; et si non obediunt dominis suis, ut debent, non est qui misereatur eorum.

Cap. LV. Pauperibus omnibus in egenorum senumque hospitiis collocatis, jubemus neminem in medio foro, vel in ecclesiis, vel in quovis alio loco panem postulare. Meus enim sermo ubique clamat : Esuriens, et sitiens, et inops veniat ad nos, et in nomine Domini idoneum accipiat subsidium solatiumque. Queruntur enim de nobis externæ gentes huc supervenientes: Non habent viscera Christiani, inquiunt; nam fratres eorum panem rogant, neque est quem eorum misereal.

Nos misereat fratrum nostrorum, præsertim vero magistrorum et dominorum.

Cap. LVI. Quotquot igitur inscripti sunt, quibus sibi opus est accipiant, neque prorsus quidquam postulent. Si quis deprehensus fuerit postulans, octodecin fustium verberibus multatus in senum hospitio includatur, admoneaturque egenorum hospitii præfectus ne eum deinceps hospitio exire sinat. Qui autem non inscriptus est, coram nobis adducatur, et cum eo misericorditer agemus. Qui autem eleemosynas facere volunt, in egenorum et senum hospitia abeuntes, ibi sua beneficia conferant. Si quis forte obvium habeat tacenten et ambulantem pauperem, neque clamitantem, sed opus aliquod quærentein et facere volentem, huic subvenire jubemus.

Cap. LVII. Omnia urbis ædificia, cum sunt pulchre locata, et mirum in modum aucta sunt locationis pretia ab iis qui quondam tyrannice res Homeritarum rexerunt, Deo juvante, locationis pretia imminui jubemus. Qui solvebat novem nummos, sex præstet, similisque fat in omnibus tertiæ partis imminutio. Qui solvebat sex, det quatuor, reliquosque duos sibi habeat. Et cætera simili ratione numerentur; duas partes tribuant, tertiamque retineant; et ne quis in posterum locationum pretium augere audeat. Sed, sicut constituimus, eodem termino administrentur, neque imminutionem, neque incrementum accipientes. Quicunque vero locationis pretio supra adjicere ausus fuerit, vel muneribus quibusdam inquilinum expellere, et pro eo alium inducat, non majore licet pretio, ipse dico talem virum domi mercedem quasi auxisse,... primum publicentur omnia istius bona, et ipse, tanquam fratrum suorum osor, atque hujus præcepti nescius : Quod ab alio oderis fieri tibi, vide ne tu aliquando alteri facias, civitate ejiciatur. Si autem cujusdam ædis herus eam ad propriam utilitatem reipsa destinat, licentiam habeat quæ volue rit faciendi; sed hujus gratia, ut educat illum, inducat alium, constituto eodem locationis pretio nec totam ædem occupare audeat. Non enim permittimus, nisi sit inquilinus pugnax vir et turbu lentus, et spirans tumultum, et fratrum aut potius hominum generis odium, vel ad alia nequitiæ opera maxime proclivis.

Cap. LVIII. Quemque regionis præfectum jubemus quæ in domibus fiant multis modis inspicere. Et si delicta quædam cognoscitis facta, referte ca domi illius hero, et confestim emendantor. Si vos audire recusat, protinus nos hujusce rei per magistratum, eparchum scilicet, certiores facite.

Cap. LIX. Quivis homo famulo suo det consortem, et liber habeat conjugem suam. Et famulabus date consortes, ut habeat quisque solatium suum et non peccent. Qui autem violaverit boc religiosum præceptum nostrum, auferatur ab eo servus cælebs, pro poena, et ancilla consortem non habens, quia regni præceptum abrogavit, Homeritarumque legem contempsit. Ablata autem mancipia regio dispensatori tradantur, de quo prius mentio facta est, et sicut constituimus flet. Quod si nonnulli semetipsos defendunt dicentes, quia. Pauper sum, ait, nec possum servo meo consortem emere, respondebimus eis: Si pauper es, vende et unicum servum tuum. Propter te enim commercia, quæ fiunt singulis diebus, lascivire non sustinebimus.

Cap. LX. Volentes in virginitate vivere ne quis impediat, et castitatein servare volentibus ne quis obstet. Requirantur ab iis chirographa propria manu scriptæ, ne veteratorie hoc modo vivant, in abscondito autem iniquitatem et peccatum faciant. Verum ex chirographa capitalis poena iis immineat. Qui potest recedere, recedat. Qui autem deprehensi fuerint, poenas in chirographa edictas luant. Phariseos enim et hypocritas in Dominuta Jesum credentes esse nolumus, scientes Deo et regibus mentiri.

Cap. LXI. Omnis regionis præfectus, qui regiun illud, et a Deo jussum, præceptum non observal it cum tremore, et reverentia, et prudentia, sed negligens, vel muneribus acceptis, quae scripta sunt in hoc præcepto nostro despicere præsumet, si cognitus fuerit, jubemus eum suspensum, sinistro pede vinctum, medio foro efferri capite prono, in palo, scilicet in trabe qualibet, et sic paleæ fumo interire, ut et cæteri hoc documento admoniti erudiantur. Expedit enim scabiosum hædum unum, a grege seductum, necari, neque grex totus ovilis, ab eo inquinatus, penitus deleatur. Hoc vero fiat in eum per hyparchum. Si autem regionis præfectum hyparchus hæc nostra præcepta violantem non poena affecerit, neque exsequatur in eum hoc piissimum

53

justissimuinque præceptum nostrum, quæcunque iste passurus fuisset, ipse patiatur hyparchus, mansuetudinis nostræ indignationem incurrens.

Cap. LXII. Præfectus quisque in ditionis suæ regione negotiationes factas diligenter inspiciat, ut juste fiant. Inspiciat fora, quomodo a mercatoribus vendantur merces; atque imprimis qui vendunt eis, exteri scilicet mercatores, dispiciantur; atque ita secundum rectam justitiam merces vendantur. Sæpius enim magno pretio, sæpius parvo, sæpius mediocri emunt. In foro omnia justo pretio veneant, ut neque venditor sit sine lucro, neque pariter emptor lædatur.

Cap. LXIII. Quemvis linificem aut textorem, quemvis opificem cujusvis artis, sancta Dominica, ne unius quidem capilli opus inchoare non permittimus. Si quis hoc faciens deprehensus fuerit, jubemus in medio foro et opus ejus et operis instrumenta igne deleri.

Cap. LXIV. Qui non recipiunt familiam omnem magnis festis et sancta Dominica, et abeuntes in sancta ecclesia pariter vespere Sabhati et sanctæ Dominicæ mane, et in liturgia ejus et in vespere, ils coram tribus dignis viris bis denuntiet regionis præfectus ut divino parcant mandato. Si autem exinde non eis præscripta exsequantur, auferatur ab iis omnis eorum substantia, et dimidium fratribus in egenorum hospitio collocatis dividatur. Reliquam vero partem habeat sibi pro lucro hujus regionis præfectus, cum assedentibus ei militibus, ut majore cum studio inquisitionem perficiant de iis omnibus quæ imperamus eis.

FINIS LEGIS.

Hæc omnia in tomo novo cum scripsisset beatus archiepiscopus Gregentius, adiens religiosissimo regi Abramio dedit, quæ rex coram se jussit perlegi. Et cuin legerentur, magnopere gavisus est et spiritu exsultavit. Accedensque rex beati manus osculatus est, quibus ea scripserat, dixitque: Benedicta hæc hora Domino, in qua de te dictum est: ecce masculus natus est. Beatissimus autem regi proposuit hæc transcribi in multis aliis libellis, ut quisque regionis præfectus proprium habere posset.

Quo facto, jussit archiepiscopus omnes regionis præfectos in ecclesia convenire. Cumque rex co venisset cum senatu et omni civitate, perfecto sancto offertorio, accipiens libellum, quem propriis scripserat manibus reverendissimus archiepiscopus, regionis præfectis dixit: Venite, dilecti mei, et accipite hæc instituta e manu Domini, ut, scientes ea non a quolibet neque quovis modo facta, sed ab ipso Domino accepta, vobis in manibus tradamus. Sumensque libellos, coram omnibus legit eos. Quibus perlectis, transcriptos libellos afferri jussit; allatosque sancto altari imposuit. Quo facto, flexo genu, precatus est beatus dixitque: Tu qui corda inspicis, juste, ineffabilis, formidande, fortis, magnipotens, sancte, Domine, extende brachium tuum excelsum et sanctum, et fortem, et terribilem, et magnum. Suscipiensque hos libellos ante oculos tuos pure constitutos, partire eos servis tuis sicut olim per Moysen septuaginta viris spiritum qui erat in eo, et sicut sanctis tuis apostolis igneas linguas.

Hæc eo precante, flavit spiritus vehemens a Domino, quasi ab altari, in libellos, et sublevans eos e loco ubi erant repositi, sicut folia ventus per aera, in singulis regionis præfectis, allevans eorum sinus, eos deposuit. Facto hoc mirabili prodigio, timore et rapitu omnes astantes cum rege ejusque proceribus impleti sunt, et videre erat omnes perculsos, et dominatorem Dominum Sabaoth extensia manibus venerantes et magnificantes.

Archiepiscopus vero præfectis dixit: Videte, dilecti, quoniam a Domino Deo nostro divina in his libellis mandata accepistis. Deinceps cum timore Dei et tremore observate ea, ut et in hoc sæculo placida tranquillaque vita fruamur, Domino ipso omnipotente leges nobis dante, et in futuro vitam cui non erit finis obtineamus.

Hære et multa alia cum ad eos archiepiscopus dixit, abierunt omnes in domos suas, glorificantes Deum. Rex vero, beati archiepiscopi manu arrepta, eum ad prandiuin deduxit.

Constituti igitur præfecti post hæc in regione quam sortiti erant, sibi ante oculos præpositis regus institutis, exsequebantur cum veneratione, et tremore, et prudentia, quaecunque sibi mandatis ints præscripta erant. Et videre erat homines honestos puriores, ut scriptum est, auro puro et sincero. Ambulabant enim cum timore et tremore omnes, scriptaque in regiis libellis celeriter plerique exsequebantur inviti et nolentes, ita ut impleretur a propheta dictus divinus sermo : Non est ruina maceriæ, neque clamor, neque transitus in plateis eorum. Et postea: Beatum dixerunt populum, ait, cui hæc sunt : et beatus populus, cujus Dominus Deus ejus.

Quæ cum ita fierent, et ita consequerentur, rexque propterea Dominum laudaret, neque quidquam injuste agere auderent proceres ejus, omne que infinita lætitia exsultarent, supervenerunt et Judæi, sicut eis præscriptum fuerat, exacto jam quadraginta dierum spatio.

Cum igitur ad disputandum convenissent, rexque meminisset, apparatu in theatro facto (aula autem illud maxima et prinia regiarum ædium superest), hic igitur apparatu facto, omnibusque cohortibus congregatis, etc.

The Scriptorium Project is the work of a small group of lay people of various apostolic churches who are interested in the preservation, transmission, and translation of the works of the early and medieval church. Our efforts are to make the works of the church fathers accessible to anyone who might have an interest in Christian antiquities and the theological, philosophical, and moral writings that have become the bedrock of Western Civilization.

To-date, our releases have pulled from the Greek, Syriac, Georgian, Latin, Celtic, Ethiopian, and Coptic traditions of Christianity, and have been pulled from sundry local traditions and languages.

www.ingramcontent.com/pod-product-compliance
Lightning Source LLC
LaVergne TN
LVHW061603070526
838199LV00077B/7155